"This is hallowed ground, the field of dreams for tennis players. It's great. It's legendary."

—James Blake on Wimbledon

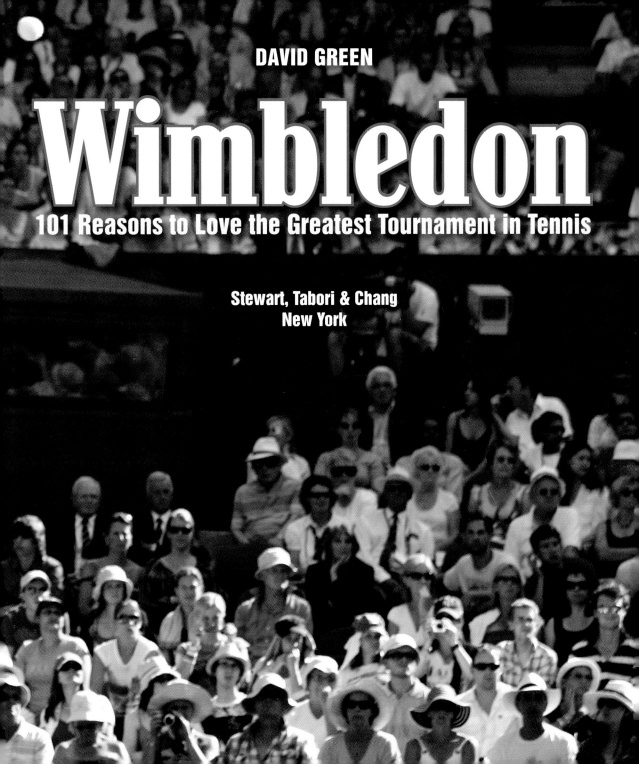

DAVID GREEN

Wimbledon

101 Reasons to Love the Greatest Tournament in Tennis

Stewart, Tabori & Chang
New York

Introduction

Wimbledon has always held a special place in my heart, since I discovered the joy of tennis as a teenager.

I grew up in a sports-centric family. My father, Ron Green, was one of the best sportswriters in the business and still contributes occasionally to the *Charlotte Observer,* even though he's now in his 80s. My brother Ron Jr. followed in his footsteps, and is an accomplished, award-winning journalist in his own right. Together, we spent countless wonderful hours playing and watching sports.

One of our favorite events was and still is Wimbledon. There's nothing quite like it, certainly not in tennis. Like The Masters in golf, there's something about the place, the traditions, and the prestige of The Championships that transcends all other events.

There's the grass and the rain, British royalty and celebrity spectators, strawberries and cream and champagne, and the best at their best on the hallowed grounds of the oldest and most prestigious venue in tennis.

The passing years and decades have brought us a steady stream of superstars and star-crossed challengers; triumph and failure; and many epic, unforgettable matches and moments. The one I remember the most, the match that made the biggest impression on me personally, was "The Tie Break" between Björn Borg and John McEnroe in 1980. Never was I more riveted while watching a match. And what a glorious match it was. Nail-biting, excruciating drama, with the final result in doubt until the very end.

Like so many others, I wanted to be Borg, with the long hair, scruffy beard, striking teen-idol looks, killer forehand, and indefatigable determination. And when he outlasted McEnroe, 8–6, in the fifth set for his fifth consecutive Wimbledon title, I was ecstatic. I felt like I had just won Wimbledon— and then I went to the courts with my friends to pound hundreds of topspin forehands and two-handed backhands.

Every Wimbledon fortnight provides special moments that will always live in our hearts. And everyone who is a fan of tennis reserves a place for that one moment that transcends them all. Perhaps you'll be reminded of your moment in the pages that follow. Enjoy the journey.

Björn Borg

1
Tennis Anyone?

The All England Croquet Club was originally founded in 1868, and land for the club was leased a year later in Wimbledon, a small hamlet along the London and South Western Railway not far from London. The modest parcel was sandwiched between the rail line and Worple Road, and it would remain the home of the club until 1922.

Lawn tennis was introduced at the club in 1875, and in 1877 the name was changed to the All England Croquet and Lawn Tennis Club. The first championship, held in July, featured a field of 22 competitors and was won by Spencer Gore, who defeated William Marshall in the final, 6–1, 6–2, 6–4. Interestingly, the tournament was staged to raise money for the repair of a broken pony roller, used to care for the croquet lawns.

J. H. Walsh, editor of *The Field* and chairman of the inaugural meeting at which the club was formed, provided the trophy—a silver "challenge cup" worth 25 guineas.

Right: The original Challenge Cup, first presented in 1877, and an illustration from the first championship.

"Grass is for cows."

— Ivan Lendl

2

The Grass

Grass. It defines Wimbledon—the only Grand Slam tournament played on the surface. Each year, the club reseeds and prepares each court, using 100 percent rye grass, which is then cut and rolled each day to a height of 8 millimeters for play. The surface is unique. The ball tends to skid on contact and bounce less than on other surfaces. Plus, it gets slippery when wet. And despite the best efforts of Wimbledon's extraordinary grounds crew, there's always the possibility of a bad bounce.

So players need to be able to react quickly if they want to succeed at tennis' greatest venue. Obviously, some players, such as Roger Federer and Steffi Graf, have enjoyed great success, while others, such as Ivan Lendl, have despised its idiosyncrasies. Lendl became so frustrated with the surface that he once pulled out of the tournament claiming he was allergic to grass. He was then seen playing golf a few days later.

3

The Rules

Lawn tennis developed from two games that were popular in Europe as far back as the sixteenth century: rackets and real tennis, or jeu de paume. Many of the best players in the early days of lawn tennis played one or both of these games.

When the All England Croquet and Lawn Tennis Club decided to host its first men's championship in 1877, Henry Jones (the referee), Julian Marshall, and C. G. Heathcote set about framing the official rules for the competition. They agreed upon the 15/30/40/deuce/advantage scoring system used in real tennis; provided two serves per point, should the server fail to put the ball in play on the first attempt; and set the court size at 78 by 27 feet, which to this day remains the size of an official singles court. The net height was set significantly higher than it is today—5 feet at the posts, angling down to 3 feet 3 inches at the center. In 1882, the net height was reduced to 3 feet 6 inches at the posts, the height that is still used today.

John Hartley

4

The Challenge Round

In 1878, it was decided that the defending champion, or holder, did not have to play through the All-Comers round, and instead had to play only the winner of the All-Comers competition in the Challenge Round to defend his title. This method of deciding the champion lasted until 1922 and made it much easier for the holder to retain his title.

5

The Vicar of Burneston

The Reverend John Hartley, vicar of Burneston, in North Yorkshire, entered the third men's lawn tennis championship in 1879 apparently not expecting to advance to the latter stages of the competition. He had neglected to schedule a replacement for regular Sunday services at Burneston, and when he emerged victorious in his quarterfinal match on Saturday, he took the train home, performed Sunday services, and returned on Monday to participate in the semifinals. Victorious there, Hartley then won the All-Comers final against Vere Thomas St. Leger Goold, 6–2, 6–4, 6–2, and was subsequently crowned champion by default when defending champion Frank Hadow did not defend his title in the Challenge Round. Hartley successfully retained his title in 1880 with a four-set win over Herbert Lawford. Hartley was then dispatched in record fashion by William Renshaw in 1881. The final lasted only 37 minutes, the shortest men's final in Wimbledon history.

Goold, along with his wife, was later convicted of the murder of Emma Levin in Monte Carlo in 1907, and he died in 1909 while serving his sentence on Devil's Island.

6
The Renshaw Twins

When William Renshaw defeated defending champ John Hartley in the 1881 Challenge Round, it began an unprecedented era of dominance by William and his twin brother, Ernest. After his 6–0, 6–1, 6–1 demolition of Hartley, William went on to win five more titles in succession, and seven in all, his last coming in 1889. William's six consecutive men's singles titles are a record that still stands today, and his total of seven is tied with Pete Sampras for the most ever.

Ernest was the unfortunate victim of William's dominance in three Challenge Rounds, in 1882, 1883, and 1889, losing the 1882 and 1883 matches in five sets. Ernest won his only Wimbledon championship in 1888 with a three-set sweep of titleholder Herbert Lawford, who had previously defeated Ernest twice in the All-Comers final, in 1885 and 1887.

In all, the Renshaw twins won eight of nine men's singles championships from 1881 to 1889. When men's doubles were made an official event in 1884, they dominated there as well, winning five of the first six titles, from 1884 to 1889.

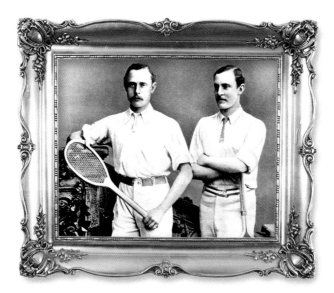

William and
Ernest Renshaw

Ladies' Day

At the suggestion of referee Henry Jones, the All England Lawn Tennis Club, renamed in 1882, added a ladies' singles championship in 1884. Maud Watson, a 19-year-old from Harrow, London, defeated her older sister, Lillian, in the final, 6–8, 6–3, 6–3, to win the first ladies' championship from a field of 13. Watson successfully defended her title in 1885 with a 6–1, 7–5 defeat of Blanche Bingley.

That was just the beginning for Bingley, however. She returned to finals in 1886, easily knocking off Watson, 6–3, 6–3. It was the first of six titles in 13 finals appearances for Bingley, who married Commander George Hillyard, later the club secretary, in 1888 and became Blanche Hillyard. Those 13 ladies' singles finals remain a record to this day, as are the 14 years between her first title and her last, in 1900, at the age of 36. Five of Hillyard's Challenge Round losses came at the hands of the legendary Lottie Dod. Hillyard continued to compete at Wimbledon until 1912, making 24 appearances in all.

Blanche Bingley Hillyard

Lottie Dod

8

Lottie Dod

Charlotte "Lottie" Dod was one of the most dominant players ever to grace the hallowed grounds of Wimbledon. At the tender age of 15, she won her first ladies' singles championship, in 1887, defeating defending champion Blanche Bingley in the Challenge Round, 6–2, 6–0. She remains the youngest champion ever to win a singles title at Wimbledon.

Dod went on to win four more singles titles, in 1888 and 1891–93, electing to skip the tournament in 1889 and 1890. In the five tournaments in which Dod competed, she lost only one set, in 1893, to Blanche Hillyard, who was her opponent in all five finals. Her prowess extended to other sports as well: Dod won two women's national field hockey championships, in 1899 and 1900; captured a silver medal in archery at the 1908 Olympics in London; and won the women's British national golf championship, held at Troon, in 1904.

9

Mr. X

As the story goes, Dr. Joshua Pim, a respected physician from Ireland, didn't want folks to know he was competing at Wimbledon; therefore in 1893, when he won the first of back-to-back championships after consecutive runner-up finishes, he played under the name Mr. X.

"When I am within a point or two of losing a game, I do feel very determined and remember that I must keep a strict command over myself."

—Lottie Dod

10

Big Do and Little Do

Reginald "Big Do" and Laurence "Little Do" Doherty are considered by many to be the first international stars in tennis. Between 1897 and 1906, the two handsome brothers from Wimbledon won nine singles titles and eight doubles titles between them. Reggie won four straight singles titles, from 1897 to 1900, followed by Laurie's streak of five straight, from 1902 to 1906. No other man won five straight singles titles until Björn Borg, from 1976 to 1980. Despite the brothers' dominance, they met only once in the Challenge Round, in 1898, when "Big Do" outlasted his little brother in five sets, 6–3, 6–3, 2–6, 5–7, 6–1. They were equally indomitable in doubles, winning every title but one from 1897 to 1905, finishing as runners-up in 1902 and 1906. Laurie's 13 combined Wimbledon titles is the men's record. The Dohertys also won four Davis Cup titles for Britain.

Charlotte Sterry versus
Agnes Morton, ladies'
singles final, 1908

Charlotte Cooper Sterry

Another five-time Wimbledon ladies' singles champion, Charlotte Cooper won her first title in 1895, when she defeated Helen Jackson in the All-Comers final, 7–5, 8–6. Titleholder Blanche Hillyard did not defend in 1895, relinquishing the title to Cooper in a walkover. Cooper went on to win subsequent championships in 1896, 1898, 1901, and 1908 at the age of 37, making her the oldest women's singles champion in Wimbledon history. An 11-time finalist, she married Alfred Sterry in 1901 and continued to play at Wimbledon, reaching the All-Comers final for the last time in 1912 at the age of 41, then played her last match in 1919, when she was 48. Cooper also earned two gold medals in the 1900 Olympics in Paris, winning the women's singles title as well as the mixed doubles with Reginald Doherty.

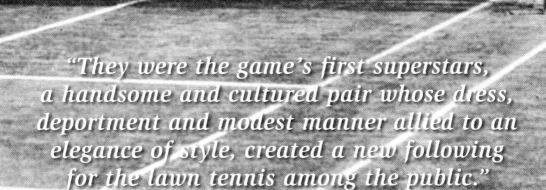

"They were the game's first superstars, a handsome and cultured pair whose dress, deportment and modest manner allied to an elegance of style, created a new following for the lawn tennis among the public."

—John Barrett, *Wimbledon: The Official History of the Championships,* on the Doherty brothers

Arthur Gore

12

Arthur Gore

Gore has a few claims to fame. He's the only man ever to beat one of the Doherty brothers in the finals at Wimbledon (when they weren't playing each other), and he's also the oldest winner ever of a singles championship at Wimbledon. Gore ended Reggie Doherty's four-year reign as men's singles champ with a 4–6, 7–5, 6–4, 6–4 victory in 1901. He didn't reach the Challenge Round again until 1908, winning his second title in a walkover after defeating H. R. Barrett in five sets in the All-Comers final. Then, in 1909, Gore claimed his third and final title when he beat Major J. G. Ritchie, 6–8, 1–6, 6–2, 6–2, 6–2, at the age of 41. He also won the men's doubles championship that year, with Barrett as his partner, and won two gold medals in the 1908 Olympics, in men's singles and doubles, again with Barrett. Gore served as club president in 1911 and played competitively until 1927.

13

Slazenger

From the white, hand-sewn, wool cloth–covered rubber balls used in the days of the Doherty brothers and Dorothea Douglass to the high-tech models played today, only one brand of tennis ball has been used at Wimbledon since 1902 — Slazenger. More than 50,000 balls are currently supplied each year in a partnership that knows no equal in sports.

Yellow tennis balls were first introduced by the International Tennis Federation (ITF) in 1972, but it wasn't until 1986 that they were first put in play at Wimbledon. Easier to see, especially for television viewers, the yellow balls have now made white tennis balls a distant memory.

Dorothea Lambert Chambers

14

Dorothea Lambert Chambers

Only Martina Navratilova (9) and Helen Wills Moody (8) won more ladies' singles titles at Wimbledon. Dorothea Douglass, a vicar's daughter from Ealing who became Mrs. Robert Lambert Chambers in 1907, won seven championships in 12 years, from 1903 to 1914, and reached the finals in four other championships, in 1905, 1907, 1919, and 1920. She lost only one set — her first in 1903 versus Ethel Thomson Larcombe — in her seven wins. Her 6–0, 6–0 demolition of Dora Boothby in 1911 is the only "whitewash" in Wimbledon finals history. In 1919, at the age of 40, Lambert Chambers held two match points at 6–5 against the international star Suzanne Lenglen, but lost the set and match 9–7 in the third.

15

May in June

With the popularity of tennis spreading around the globe, particularly in the United States, it was inevitable that an American would eventually be crowned Wimbledon champion. The first to claim a title was May Sutton, in 1905. Sutton, who had won the U.S. Championships in 1904 at the age of 18, cruised by two-time defending champion Dorothea Douglass, 6–3, 6–4, and then repeated the feat two years later, winning 6–1, 6–4. It was Douglass, however, who got the better of Sutton in 1906, winning 6–3, 9–7.

Sutton caused a minor stir in 1905 when she rolled up the cuffs of her blouse, exposing her wrists (gasp!). It also should be noted that while Sutton is considered the first American to hold a Wimbledon title, she was born in Plymouth, England, and moved to California at the age of six.

1908 Olympics men's doubles championship
Inset: Anthony Wilding

16
The Olympics

When the 2012 Summer Olympics are held in London, Wimbledon will play host to the Olympic tennis tournament. The All England Club also hosted the tennis events during the 1908 Olympics. British players swept all six events: men's and women's singles, men's and women's indoor singles, men's doubles, and men's indoor doubles.

17
Go Wilding

Anthony Wilding is the only New Zealander ever to win a singles title at Wimbledon. But Wilding didn't win just one. He won four straight championships from 1910 to 1913, and had a shot at a fifth in 1914 but lost in straight sets to Norman Brookes. Described as handsome and regal, the barrister from Christchurch was never stretched to a fifth set in his four championship matches. Wilding also captured four men's doubles championships, in 1907, 1908, 1910, and 1914—two each with Norman Brooks and Major J. G. Ritchie. His career might have been even more impressive, but Wilding was killed in action in France during World War I, in 1915.

18

Triple Crown Winners

At Wimbledon, the Triple Crown refers to winners of the singles, doubles, and mixed doubles championships in the same year. Only three men have completed the feat: Don Budge (1937, 1938); Bobby Riggs (1939); and Frank Sedgman (1952). Five women have captured the Triple Crown: Suzanne Lenglen (1920, 1922, 1925); Alice Marble (1939); Louise Brough (1948, 1950); Doris Hart (1951); and Billie Jean King (1967, 1973).

19

Suzanne Lenglen

When the championships returned to Wimbledon in 1919 after a four-year hiatus during World War I, it was Lenglen who emerged as the new star of women's tennis. The 20-year-old from France defeated 40-year-old, seven-time champion Dorothea Lambert Chambers, 10–8, 4–6, 9–7, to win the first of six titles in seven years. That would be the only time Lenglen would lose a set in seven Wimbledon finals. In fact, in the ensuing six championship matches, she lost a total of only 13 games.

Dubbed "La Divine" by the French press, Lenglen became an international star and revolutionized women's tennis, choosing to wear lighter, more stylish outfits instead of the restrictive, traditional heavy skirts worn by Lambert Chambers and other past champions. Her style and grace on the court, reflective of her training in ballet when she was a child, won her legions of fans. In addition to her six ladies' singles titles, Lenglen won six women's doubles titles with Elizabeth Ryan—the two never lost a match—and three mixed doubles titles. She was the first woman and one of only five ever to win the Triple Crown at Wimbledon, and the only player ever to accomplish the feat three times, in 1920, 1922, and 1925. The All England Lawn Tennis Club ranks her as one of the top five champions in Wimbledon history.

"She played with marvelous ease the simplest strokes in the world."

—René Lacoste
on Suzanne Lenglen

Suzanne Lenglen

Suzanne Lenglen, 1926

20

A Winning Recipe

It's hard to argue with success. Suzanne Lenglen's agility, speed, and accuracy made her nearly impossible to beat from 1919 to 1925, but she also had a secret ingredient. To boost her energy, her "Papa" tossed her brandy-soaked sugar cubes between games. She was also known to sip cognac between sets on occasion.

21

A Match to Remember

The 1919 ladies' singles final between seven-time champion Dorothea Lambert Chambers and young upstart Suzanne Lenglen is considered one of the greatest matches in Wimbledon history. With King George V and Queen Mary among the 8,000 spectators in attendance, Lenglen outlasted Chambers in a grueling first set, 10–8. Chambers fought back to take the second set, 6–4, sending the match to the third and deciding set. Lenglen quickly jumped to a 4–1 lead, but Chambers rallied, winning five of the next six games to take a 6–5 lead. Serving for the match, Chambers held two match points, but Lenglen saved both — the first a mishit off the tip of her racket that just cleared the net and died on the turf. Given a second life, she recovered and outlasted Chambers 9–7 in the final set to win her first Wimbledon singles title.

"She owned every kind of shot, plus a genius for knowing how and when to use them."

—Elizabeth Ryan on Suzanne Lenglen

22

Big Bill

Bill Tilden is widely considered to be one of the greatest tennis players ever, if not the best. Tall and athletic, "Big Bill" mixed guile and strategy with power and finesse. When he won his first Wimbledon men's singles title in 1920 over G. L. Patterson, it was the start of an incredible decade of tennis. Tilden successfully defended his title in 1921, recovering from a two-set deficit to stun Brian "Babe" Norton, 4–6, 2–6, 6–1, 6–0, 7–5, in the final. And after three consecutive losses in the semifinals, he won his third championship in 1930 at the age of 37, defeating Wilmer Allison in straight sets. The nine years between titles is the longest span in Wimbledon history.

Tilden's greatness was not limited to the grass in England. From 1920 through 1925, he won six consecutive U.S. Championships, adding a seventh in 1929. And he led the American Davis Cup team to seven straight titles from 1920 through 1926. His power, skill, and mental approach changed the game, and tennis on the lawns of Wimbledon would never be the same.

23

Elizabeth Ryan

Billie Jean King and Martina Navratilova hold the record for most Wimbledon championships overall with 20 each. Ryan is next with 19. King has six singles titles to her credit, and Navratilova has a record nine singles titles. Remarkably, Ryan won her 19 Wimbledon titles without ever winning the ladies' singles. She won a record 12 ladies' doubles championships, from 1914 through 1934 (six with Suzanne Lenglen), and a record seven mixed doubles championships from 1919 through 1932. Ryan made two appearances in the ladies' singles final, bowing to Lenglen in 1921 and Helen Wills Moody in 1930.

"The game is a science
and an art."

—Bill Tilden

24

Church Road

At the conclusion of World War I, there was a renewed interest in tennis, and the club, looking to expand its facilities, purchased a plot of land on Church Road, not far from the original site. Plans were drawn up for a new stadium court with seating for 11,000, and money was raised through the sale of debentures to help finance the construction. Although when it opened in 1922, Centre Court wasn't surrounded by the other courts as it had been at Worple Road, it retained its name. Over the years, as the facilities have been expanded, Centre Court is again roughly at the center of the Wimbledon grounds.

"This is not the end of the rain, it is not even the

Brian Viner, *The Independent*, paraphrasing Winston Churchill, 2004

The Rain

It's a rare occasion that rain doesn't interrupt play at some point during The Championships. In 1922, the first year The Championships were played at Church Road, it rained every day, and the tournament was extended to the third Wednesday—the longest it has ever run. Matches get delayed. Some are extended over the course of two days, or more. Momentum shifts. Some players get a reprieve, while others suffer a crueler fate, unable to adjust to the whims of the weather.

Despite these interruptions, Wimbledon officials work extremely hard to keep things running smoothly, expertly juggling schedules and having the courts ready for play. Court coverers train for two weeks prior to The Championships and can pull a tarp into place in about 30 seconds, keeping the courts dry and playable.

And then there are the fans. They tend to accept the rain as part of the deal, enduring delays and cancellations with smiling faces and that famous British stoicism. After all, it gives them more time to enjoy the famous strawberries and cream, sip some champagne, or warm up with some tea.

beginning of the end, but it is the end of the beginning."

26

The Royal Box

British royalty first visited The Championships in 1907, when the Prince of Wales and Princess Mary attended Saturday matches. When Queen Mary presided over the opening of the new facilities at Church Road in 1922, she set a precedent for royalty presiding over Centre Court. From 1919 through 1934, King George V and Queen Mary attended all but two championships. With the exception of 1936, Queen Mary never missed another year until her last visit, in 1957.

Up until 2003, players were required to bow or curtsy to the Royal Box when entering Centre Court, but the Duke of Kent, president of the club, revised the protocol, deeming it necessary only if the queen or Prince of Wales were in attendance. The duke and duchess are the official royal representatives and regularly make the trophy presentations at the conclusion of the matches.

27

The Draw

They still do it by hand, drawing numbers out of a cloth bag. On the Friday preceding the opening day of The Championships, the official draw is conducted, placing all unseeded players in brackets with the seeded players. There is always rampant speculation around which players got the easiest or toughest draws. That luck of the draw can make or break a player's fortnight.

Wimbledon began seeding players according to ability, regardless of nationality, in 1927 and began using computer rankings to determine seedings in 1975. The top 32 players from a field of 128 are seeded in the men's and women's singles, and the top 16 pairs are seeded in doubles. Since 1927, only two unseeded players have ever won a singles title—Boris Becker in 1985 and Goran Ivanisevic in 2001. Kurt Nielsen is the only unseeded player to reach the finals twice, losing to Vic Seixas in 1953 and Tony Trabert in 1955.

28

The Four Musketeers

From the first championship, held in 1877, through 1923, no Frenchman had ever won a men's singles title at Wimbledon. In fact, none had ever reached the final. (André Henri Gobert lost to Arthur Gore in the All-Comers final in 1912.) But that all changed in 1924, when Jean Borotra defeated fellow countryman René Lacoste in a five-set thriller, 6–1, 3–6, 6–1, 3–6, 6–4. It was the first of six straight wins by French players.

Borotra won a second title in 1926. Lacoste won championships in 1925 and 1928, and Henri Cochet held the trophy in 1927 and 1929. In 1927, Cochet lost the first two sets in each of his last three matches and saved six match points against Borotra in the final, winning the fifth set, 7–5. In all but one of those years, 1926, one of the three was also the runner-up.

The three champions and doubles expert Jacques "Toto" Brugnon were known as "The Four Musketeers." Brugnon won four men's doubles championships, two with Cochet, in 1926 and 1928, and two with Borotra, in 1932 and 1933. Borotra also won a doubles title with René Lacoste in 1925. It was a period of unprecedented dominance for the French.

Borotra was known as the "Bounding Basque" for his exuberant style and tendency to leap into the crowd while chasing down balls. Often he would then find himself in the lap of a pretty girl in the front row. With a doff of his signature blue beret and a kiss of a hand, the charming Frenchman would somewhat reluctantly return to the court for the next point.

Lacoste, nicknamed "the Crocodile," went on to design clothing and equipment for tennis. The Lacoste brand, with its signature crocodile logo, is still a popular premium brand today.

Jack Crawford, 1933
Inset: Leslie Godfree
and wife, Kitty, 1928

29
Crawford Versus Vines

The 1933 men's singles final between second-seeded Jack Crawford and top-seeded defending champion Ellsworth Vines is regarded as one of the best matches in Wimbledon history. They traded blows for five sets, with Crawford eventually conquering the world's best player at the time, 4–6, 11–9, 6–2, 2–6, 6–4. Crawford shocked everyone, including Vines, who had a punishing serve, when he broke Vines at love in the 10th and final game of the fifth set to win the match.

Vines might have won more Wimbledon titles had he not turned pro in 1934. Crawford won the first three legs of the Grand Slam in 1933 but just missed becoming the first man to complete the Grand Slam when he lost to Fred Perry in the finals of the U.S. Championships in five sets after leading two sets to one.

30
Good Chemistry

Success in doubles, like marriage, requires good chemistry. One of the best examples of that may have been in 1926 when Kitty McKane Godfree and her husband, Leslie, won the mixed doubles championship. To this day, they're the only married couple to win a mixed doubles title at Wimbledon. Kitty is probably better known as the only woman to defeat Helen Wills Moody in the ladies' singles final, in 1924. She won a second Wimbledon singles title in 1926.

31

Fred Perry

When Fred Perry defeated titleholder Jack Crawford in straight sets to claim the 1934 men's singles title, he became the first British man in 21 years to win at Wimbledon. Perry, a former world table tennis champion with a punishing forehand, went on to win the next two men's singles titles, both versus Gottfried von Cramm, to give him three straight. The third title was one of the more dominant performances in men's finals history — a 6–1, 6–1, 6–0 obliteration of von Cramm.

Perry, the last Brit to win the men's singles title at Wimbledon, or any Grand Slam title for that matter, and widely considered the last great British men's player, won eight Grand Slam singles titles overall, and was the first man ever to win all four tournaments in his career. In 1984, the All England Club named the Somerset Road entrance "Perry Gates" in his honor, and a statue of Perry now stands near Doherty Gates on Church Road.

"I didn't aspire to be a good sport; 'champion' was good enough for me."

—Fred Perry

32

Little Miss Poker Face

Nicknamed "Little Miss Poker Face" by the famed sportswriter Grantland Rice for her unchanging expression, Helen Wills Moody is one of the most dominant women's tennis players in history. She won Wimbledon's women's singles championship eight times in 12 years, from 1927 to 1938, including four in a row from 1927 to 1930. When Moody lost the second set to Dorothy Round in the 1933 final, it was the first set she had lost at Wimbledon since 1927.

For her career, she won 19 Grand Slam singles titles, including seven U.S. Championships and four French Championships, and held 31 Grand Slam titles overall, including doubles and mixed doubles. She never played in Australia.

*"Tennis is a diversion,
not a career."*

—Helen Wills Moody

The Midlands Sunday School Mistress

As a Methodist Sunday school teacher, Dorothy Round became known as the "Midlands Sunday School Mistress" because of her refusal to play matches on Sunday. Often remembered as the first woman to win a set off the legendary Helen Wills Moody at Wimbledon in six years, Round earned her own place in Wimbledon lore. Capitalizing on the absence of Moody in 1934 and 1937, she won two Wimbledon singles titles, defeating Helen Jacobs in 1934 and Jadwiga Jedrzejowska in 1937, both in three sets.

"An outstanding player in her own right, whose athleticism, grace and competitiveness invited comparison with the great Suzanne Lenglen."

—TennisForum.com on Dorothy Round

Dorothy Round. Inset: Helen Jacobs, left, and Helen Wills Moody

34

If at First...

Helen Jacobs was one of the finest American tennis players of her generation. She won the women's singles title at the U.S. Championships four consecutive years, from 1932 to 1935. But she didn't fare quite as well at Wimbledon, where she had the unfortunate luck to play during the era of Helen Wills Moody. Four times between 1929 and 1938, Moody defeated Jacobs in the women's final. Jacobs did break through in 1936, winning her only Wimbledon singles title over Hilde Sperling in three sets, 6–2, 4–6, 7–5. It should be noted that Moody didn't play that year. Jacobs was also the first woman to wear shorts at Wimbledon, in 1933.

Don Budge

Twice a semifinalist at Wimbledon, Budge broke through in 1937, winning his first of two men's singles titles, defeating Gottfried von Cramm in straight sets. That started a run of six consecutive Grand Slam singles titles for Budge. When he returned to Wimbledon to defend his title in 1938, Budge held all four Grand Slam titles at once, having won the U.S. Championships in 1937 and the Australian and French championships in 1938. Sporting one of the best back-hands in the history of the game, Budge cruised past Bunny Austin at Wimbledon, 6–1, 6–0, 6–3, then forever etched his name in tennis history by winning the U.S. Championship that same summer, becoming the first man ever to win all four Grand Slam titles in a single year. Budge is another in a long list of players who might have won more Wimbledon titles had he not chosen to turn pro in 1939.

The War Effort

When Bobby Riggs and Alice Marble each won the Triple Crown in 1939, no one had any way of knowing it would be seven long years before another Wimbledon championship took place. On October 11, 1940, 16 German bombs fell on the property, one of which flattened a corner of Centre Court. During the war, the Main Concourse was used as a parade ground for soldiers of the London Welsh and London Irish regiments as well as F Company of the Wimbledon Home Guard. The club served as a first-aid headquarters, and the car parks were plowed and planted for food production. Head groundskeeper Edwin Fuller cared for the courts, and in 1945 two sets of matches were played by teams from the Allied Forces. The official championships resumed in 1946, despite the damage to Centre Court and continued shortages of food, clothing, and gas.

Plowing of a Wimbledon car park during World War II

"Many people say to me that it was easier for a player to win the Grand Slam in my day. I always reply, 'Well, if that is so, why couldn't someone else do it?'"

—Don Budge

Gorgeous Gussie

When Gussie Moran arrived at Wimbledon in 1949 sporting lace-trimmed panties beneath her regulation white dress, she caused a major sensation. They were designed by Teddy Tinling, "callboy" at The Championships. The press dubbed the leggy Moran "Gorgeous Gussie." Stories and photos were splashed across the pages of newspapers and magazines. *Life* magazine even ran a special feature. Unfortunately for Moran and her fans, she lost in the third round.

Gussie Moran showing off her form and her lace-trimmed panties, 1949

38

Court Couturier

Teddy Tinling served as "callboy" at Wimbledon for many years, ushering players to and from the court. But his employment at the All England Club ended in 1949 when Gussie Moran wore the infamous lace-trimmed panties under the stylish frock Tinling had designed for her. Club officials may have been appalled, but the players took notice. Tinling went on to become the designer to the stars, outfitting many of the best in women's tennis with eye-catching yet functional creations, earning him the nickname "the Dior of Centre Court."

39

Wearing White

It's a tradition at Wimbledon. The players' dress code requires them to wear clothing that is predominantly white. Although splashes of color and sponsors' logos are allowed, they can't be prominent. The appropriately named Anne White stretched the limits of the code when she wore a white unitard in 1985. Thankfully, it didn't catch on. Andre Agassi was forced to forgo his denim cutoffs over pink cycling shorts. And Bethanie Mattek caused a stir in 2006 when she wore what she described as a "soccer-themed" outfit, featuring a tube top stretched over a halter top, skimpy gym shorts, and knee-high tube socks. "I pretty much went with my gut," she said. "Hopefully, it was good." It wasn't.

40

Miss Fancy Pants

In 1958, Wimbledon officials banned Karol Fageros from competition after she wore gold lamé underpants during the French Open. Fageros agreed to cover her underpants with white lace, which apparently was less offensive to club officials, and she was allowed to play.

41

Louise Brough

A classic serve-and-volleyer from California, Brough won Wimbledon's women's singles title for three consecutive years, from 1948 to 1950, and won a fourth championship in 1955. In the 1955 final against third-seed Beverly Baker Fleitz, Brough trailed 4–5 in both sets but came back to win 7–5, 8–6. She was also a four-time winner in mixed doubles and a five-time champion in ladies' doubles. Brough and ladies' doubles partner Margaret Osborne du Pont formed a nearly unbeatable pair, winning four titles from 1948 to 1954. Even more impressive, they won nine straight U.S. doubles titles from 1942 to 1950 and three more from 1955 to 1957. Brough won a total of 35 Grand Slam titles in a career that spanned more than 20 years.

42

Little Mo

The diminutive Californian Maureen "Little Mo" Connolly took over where Louise Brough left off, winning three consecutive ladies' singles titles from 1952 to 1954, beating Brough twice, in 1952 and 1954. She was only 17 when she won her first Wimbledon title, in 1952. The following year, Connolly defeated Doris Hart on her way to winning the Grand Slam—the first woman to achieve the feat. Fiercely determined and unflinching, Connolly intimidated her opponents despite her size and used a powerful baseline game to overwhelm them. Her career was cut short when she broke her leg after being thrown from a horse when she was only 20. More tragedy followed: Connolly died of cancer in 1969 at the age of 34.

Maureen Connolly receives the champion's trophy from the Duchess of Kent as Louise Brough looks on, 1952.

Althea Gibson receives a kiss from runner-up Darlene Hard, 1957.
Inset: Maria Bueno

43

Althea Gibson

Referred to by some as "the Jackie Robinson of tennis," Gibson was the first African American to win a Grand Slam event, capturing the 1956 French Championships title over Angela Mortimer. Gibson then won her first of three ladies' doubles titles at Wimbledon that same year, paired with Angela Buxton. In 1957, Gibson defeated doubles partner Darlene Hard, 6–3, 6–2, to win her first singles title at The Championships—while she and Hard won the ladies' doubles. And then Gibson went on to win a second consecutive singles title in 1958, with a straight-set victory over Angela Mortimer, and added a third straight doubles title, this time paired with Maria Bueno.

44

Muy Bueno

Maria Bueno prowled the court with a wonderful mix of feline grace and ferocity, painting her strokes with the style of an artist. Strikingly elegant in her Teddy Tinling dresses, Bueno was a joy to behold. The lithe Brazilian was the winner of three Wimbledon ladies' singles titles, in 1959, 1960, and 1964, losing in the finals in 1965 and 1966. Her first win, versus Darlene Hard, came when Bueno was only 19 years old, and her last was a three-set masterpiece against the great Margaret Smith (Court). Bueno also won five women's doubles titles at Wimbledon between 1958 and 1966, playing with such greats as Althea Gibson (1958), Darlene Hard (1960, 1963), Billie Jean King (1965), and Nancy Richey (1966).

"Maria's backhand was a poem of sweeping grace."

—C. M. Jones, *Lawn Tennis* magazine

Rod Laver

"I remain unconvinced
that there ever was
a better player than
Rod Laver."

—Bud Collins

45

The Rocket

Australian Rod Laver is the only player ever to win the tennis Grand Slam twice. After losing in the men's finals in the previous two years at Wimbledon, "the Rocket" finally broke through in 1961, defeating Charles McKinley in straight sets for his first Wimbledon title. Laver followed that up with a second consecutive championship in 1962—a straight-set blitz of fellow Aussie Martin Mulligan that gave him the third leg of his first Grand Slam.

Laver turned pro after completing his first Slam and didn't play Wimbledon again until the Open era arrived in 1968. With one of the most technically sound all-around games ever, Laver, who kept himself in peak physical condition, was able to win his third title that year, defeating fellow Aussie Tony Roche in straight sets. When Laver arrived at Wimbledon in 1969, he was halfway to another Slam. He didn't waste the opportunity, dispatching yet another Aussie, John Newcombe, for his fourth men's singles title. Newcombe did manage to win one set off him, however. Laver went on to win the U.S. Open that year and claim his second Grand Slam. He also set a record for consecutive matches won at Wimbledon, 31, which was broken in 1980 by Björn Borg.

46

The Open Era

From its humble beginnings in 1877 through 1967, The Championships at Wimbledon were contested exclusively by amateurs. For many years it was irrelevant, since there was no organized tour for professionals. But as more and more of the best players turned pro during the 1950s and 1960s, it became clear that things would have to change if Wimbledon and the other major tennis events were going to continue to attract the best players in the world. So, in 1968, the All England Club, along with the directors of the other Grand Slam events, elected to allow professionals to play in the tournaments for the first time.

47

Gracious Hosts

When Angela Mortimer defeated Christine Truman, 4–6, 6–4, 7–5, in the 1961 ladies' singles final, it marked the first time since 1914 that two Brits played for the title . . . and the last. Think that's amazing? The last time two British men played for the singles title was in 1909, when Arthur Gore beat Major J. G. Ritchie. It's an impressive display of politeness on the part of the Brits, always letting guests win on their home court like that.

48

Roy Emerson

Aussie Roy Emerson won back-to-back men's singles titles in 1964 and 1965, each time defeating Fred Stolle. Considered by many to be the fastest, fittest tennis player ever, Emerson had a shot at a rare third straight title in 1966, but injured himself when he crashed into the umpire's chair while chasing a ball. He ended up losing in the quarterfinals to Owen Davidson.

Emerson won 12 Grand Slam singles titles overall, a record that stood until 2000 when it was broken by Pete Sampras. Emerson also won 16 Grand Slam doubles titles, including three at Wimbledon, in 1959, 1961, and 1971, giving him a total of 28 Grand Slam titles, the all-time record for men.

"A traditional fixture at Wimbledon is the way the BBC-TV commentary box fills up with British players eliminated in the early rounds."

—Clive James

Todd Woodbridge, foreground, and Mark Woodforde, 1997

49

Aussies Rule

From 1948 to 2000, the world witnessed a run of dominance in men's doubles that is unmatched. During that time, Aussies won an incredible 28 titles. Sure, British men won every doubles crown up until 1907, but just about everyone who played in the early days was from Britain.

From 1948 to 1971, the Australians claimed 18 titles in 24 years, led by such great players as John Newcombe, Tony Roche, Roy Emerson, Lew Hoad, and Rod Laver. Newcombe and Roche won five titles from 1965 through 1974. Then, from 1993 to 2000, Todd Woodbridge and Mark Woodforde—"the Woodies"—won six titles in eight years, including five in a row starting in 1993. Woodbridge went on to win three more titles with Swede Jonas Björkman making him the holder of the most men's doubles titles with nine.

John Newcombe

The Presidents

1938 D BUDGE
1939 R L RIGGS
1946 Y PETRA
1947 J KRAMER
1948 R FALKENBURG
1949 F R SCHROEDER
1950 B PATTY
1951 R SAVITT
1952 F A SEDGMAN
1953 V SEIX

50

Ken Rosewall

Rosewall, another of the great Australian players of his generation, won eight Grand Slam singles titles, but none of them came on the lawns of Wimbledon. Four times, spanning 20 years, Rosewall tried in vain to win the one title that would give him a career Grand Slam, but it was not to be. In 1954, he lost in four sets to 11th-seeded upstart Jaroslav Drobný. Two years later, countryman Lew Hoad topped Rosewall in four sets. More than a decade passed and it looked as if Rosewall's time had come and gone, but he returned to the finals in 1970, where he lost a heartbreaker to fellow Aussie John Newcombe in five sets. And yet, the quest was still not over. In 1974, approaching the age of 40, Rosewall made it back to one last final, only to have his hopes swept away in straight sets by a brash young American by the name of Jimmy Connors. Rosewall did win two men's doubles titles at Wimbledon, in 1953 and 1956, with Hoad.

51

John Newcombe

Along with six men's doubles championships at Wimbledon, Newcombe won the men's singles title three times, in 1967, 1970, and 1971. With a solid overall game that featured an overpowering forehand and devastating overhead, Newcombe cruised to a straight-set victory over Wilhelm Bungert in 1967, in the last amateur contest before Wimbledon opened its doors to professionals in 1968. His wins versus fellow Aussie Ken Rosewall in 1970 and American Stan Smith in 1971 were both five-set classics. Newcombe was banned from defending his title in 1972 by the International Tennis Federation (ITF) because of his membership in World Championship Tennis (WCT).

"At Wimbledon, the ladies are simply the candles on the cake."

—John Newcombe

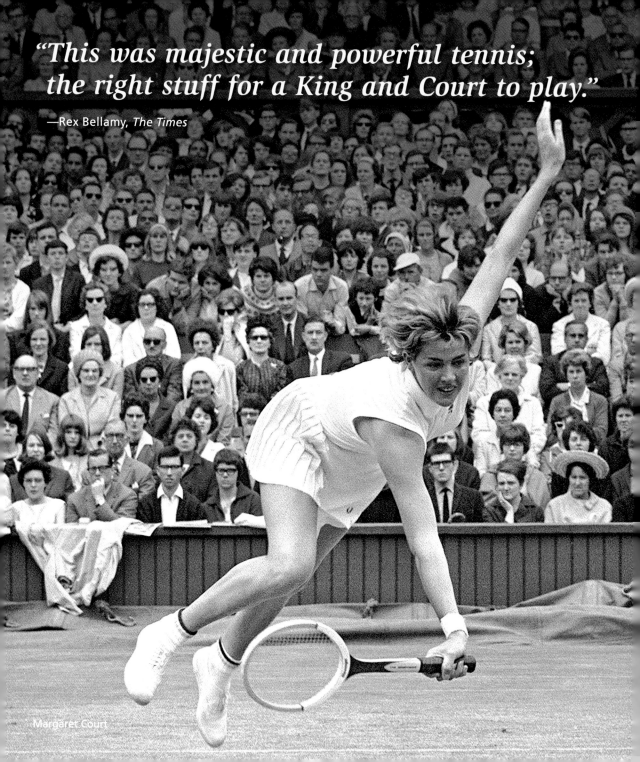

"This was majestic and powerful tennis; the right stuff for a King and Court to play."

—Rex Bellamy, *The Times*

Margaret Court

52

Margaret Court

Court holds the all-time record for Grand Slam victories with 62, including a record 24 singles titles, 19 doubles titles, and a record 19 mixed doubles titles. A fitness fanatic who could overpower her opponents, the Aussie won three Wimbledon singles championships—an impressive total by any account, but a somewhat surprisingly low number for a player of her immense talents.

Before her marriage to Barrymore Court in 1967, Court was known by her maiden name, Margaret Smith. In 1963, Smith knocked off Billie Jean Moffitt (King), 6–3, 6–4, for her first title. Maria Bueno defeated Smith in the final the following year, but Smith returned the favor in 1965, edging Bueno, 6–4, 7–5. Five years later, after her marriage, Court returned to the final, where she outlasted King in an epic match, 14–12, 11–9, widely considered to be the best women's final ever.

Court went on to complete the Grand Slam in 1970, making her only the second woman in history (at the time) to achieve the feat. She is also the only player ever to win all 12 Grand Slam events twice—singles, doubles, and mixed doubles in each championship.

53

Court Reigns over King

The two titans of the women's game met in an unforgettable final in 1970. Margaret Court played with an injured ankle numbed with novocaine, and Billie Jean King fought a balky knee that required surgery the following week. Despite their infirmities, King and Court took 26 games to decide the first set, with Court breaking King to win 14–12—the longest first set in Wimbledon finals history. Not much changed in the second set. The two traded games like boxers trading jabs, punching and counterpunching until the 20th game, when Court finally landed the decisive blow on her sixth match point with King netting her shot, giving Court the set 11–9. The two-set match took an incredible 2 hours and 28 minutes to play and set a record for most games ever in a women's final.

Billie Jean King

Most tennis buffs will tell you that King is the greatest American-born women's tennis player ever. Her success at Wimbledon certainly supports that. In 1966, King won the first of three consecutive Wimbledon singles titles and went on to capture six in a 10-year span. She was even more successful in women's doubles, winning 10 championships between 1961 and 1979, five with partner Rosie Casals. The last doubles victory gave her a record 20 Wimbledon titles, which also include four mixed doubles championships. A relentless competitor, constantly on the attack, King won her titles in an era that featured many of the best women's players ever, including Margaret Court, Maria Bueno, Chris Evert, and a young Martina Navratilova, making her record-setting achievements all the more impressive.

> ## "Victory is fleeting. Losing is forever."
>
> —Billie Jean King

Billie Jean King, right, celebrates her 20th Wimbledon title with doubles partner Martina Navratilova, center, and the Duchess of Kent, 1979.

Charlie Pasarell, left, and Pancho Gonzalez

55

Pancho Versus Charlie

At the time, it was the longest match ever. Over two days during the summer of 1969, the great Pancho Gonzales and Charlie Pasarell played a match like no other. In the era before tie breaks—in fact, it was the match that led to the creation of tie breaks—the 41-year-old Gonzales played a 112-game tug-of-war with the much younger Pasarell for an amazing 5 hours and 12 minutes. In the end, after saving seven match points, Gonzales outlasted Pasarell, winning 22–24, 1–6, 16–14, 6–3, 11–9. Gonzales went on to win his next two matches before falling to Arthur Ashe in four sets in the fourth round.

56

The Graveyard

Over the years, Court 2 became known as "the graveyard of champions." Many notable upsets have taken place there, including 145th-ranked George Basti's surprising second-round defeat of seven-time champion Pete Sampras in 2002, qualifier Doug Flach's shocking first-round win over 1992 champion Andre Agassi in 1996, and defending champion Jimmy Connors' stunning loss to Kevin Curren in 1983.

The old court that gave so many prominent players nightmares has itself been laid to rest. A new Court 2 now stands where Court 13 used to be, and another new court is currently being built on the old "graveyard."

"I think I was better off staying home."

—Serena Williams after losing to 83rd-ranked Jill Craybas on Court 2 in 2005

57

Jimmy Connors

He was brash, prone to juvenile displays of emotion, and even got himself booed on Centre Court after he declined to participate in the Parade of Champions on the 100th anniversary of The Championships in 1977, but Connors could play. When he was only 21, he destroyed 39-year-old Ken Rosewall with his all-out, aggressive style, 6–1, 6–1, 6–4, to win his first men's singles title at Wimbledon, in 1974. Connors returned to defend his title in 1975, but lost to Arthur Ashe in a shocker. Most had thought Connors would simply overpower the underdog Ashe. Then, after consecutive losses to Björn Borg in the finals in 1977 and 1978, Connors won his second Wimbledon crown in 1982, besting John McEnroe in a classic five-set match. Love him or hate him, Connors certainly left his mark on Wimbledon and the game of tennis.

58

An Old-Fashioned Ashe-Kickin'

Jimmy Connors and Arthur Ashe couldn't have been more different. Connors was the young colt, full of piss and vinegar, and Ashe was the gentleman of tennis. When Connors refused to represent the United States in the Davis Cup, Ashe described him as "unpatriotic." Connors sued for libel but later dropped the suit. He also sued the Association of Tennis Professionals (ATP)— Ashe was president—in 1974 for banning Connors from the French Open because he signed a contract to play World Team Tennis. So there was no love lost when the two met in the 1975 Wimbledon final. Connors was expected to cruise past the overmatched Ashe. But using a combination of guile and savvy, drop shots and change of pace, Ashe kept Connors off balance the entire match and produced one of Wimbledon's more shocking upsets, winning 6–1, 6–1, 5–7, 6–4, making Ashe the first African American man to win Wimbledon. Connors, perhaps humbled ever so slightly, dropped his lawsuit against the ATP.

Jimmy Connors and
Chris Evert, 1974

59
Chris Evert

The pretty, ponytailed "girl next door" from Florida might have looked like a pushover when she first appeared on the professional tennis scene at age 16, but Evert was anything but that. Tough and determined, with nerves of steel, Evert earned the nickname "the Ice Maiden" as she became a dominant force in women's tennis in the 1970s. After losing her first Wimbledon final to Billie Jean King in 1973, Evert came back to win three singles titles in 1974, 1976, and 1981, the first coming when she was only 19 years old. Her two-handed backhand revolutionized tennis and led her to 10 appearances in the ladies' singles final over a span of only 13 years. Five times she fell victim to the brilliance of Martina Navratilova. The two rivals paired to win the ladies' doubles title in 1976.

60
Love Match

American tennis stars Chris Evert and Jimmy Connors had a popular if brief romance in the 1970s that led to their engagement. Things peaked at Wimbledon in 1974 when they each won their respective singles titles. Plans were made for a wedding that fall, but it was called off and the "Love Match" ended.

"You're always striving to play that perfect match."

—Chris Evert

Ilie Nastase, 1974
Inset: Björn Borg, 1972

61

The Bucharest Buffoon

Fiery Romanian Ilie Nastase was one of the best players in the world in the early 1970s, earning the number one ranking in 1973, so maybe the "Bucharest Buffoon" moniker was a bit unfair. He lost a heartbreaker to Stan Smith in an epic five-set final at Wimbledon in 1972 and was Björn Borg's first victim, in 1976. In between, he won the men's doubles title with Jimmy Connors in 1973. But Nastase's antics often overshadowed his artistry on the court. One of Nastase's most memorable moments came in a fourth-round match versus Dick Stockton in 1974, when he grabbed a fan's umbrella and playfully held it over his head while awaiting Stockton's serve in an attempt to get the umpire to halt play because of a light mist. The ploy failed and Stockton went on to win the match in four sets, but it's the umbrella that everyone remembers.

62

Chimbledon

Wimbledon began hosting junior events, for players under the age of 18, in 1947. Over the years, this tournament has become known as Chimbledon (Children's Wimbledon). In 1975, these events were given championship status. Some past champions who also won Wimbledon as juniors include Björn Borg, Stefan Edberg, Roger Federer, and Martina Hingis.

63

For She's a Jolly Good Fellow

To celebrate the 100th anniversary of the first championship in 1877, Wimbledon held a special ceremony honoring past champions. For the first time in 15 years, the queen was in attendance, celebrating her Silver Jubilee—25 years on the throne. And England's Virginia Wade, playing in her 16th Championship, provided the perfect ending to a very special fortnight.

Hopes were high that a British woman might win the singles title that year, but much of the focus was on fellow Brit Sue Barker, as well as international stars Chris Evert and Martina Navratilova. Wade, who was nearing the end of her career, made a surprising run and dispatched defending champion Chris Evert in the semifinals, 6–2, 4–6, 6–1. All of Britain held their collective breath as Wade and Betty Stove (who had beaten Barker in the semifinals) battled for the title. Wade lost the first set but then found her game and overpowered Stove in the final two sets for a 4–6, 6–3, 6–1 victory. The crowd went crazy. As the queen, clad in a pink hat and coat, presented Wade with the champion's Venus Rosewater Dish, they spontaneously serenaded her with "For She's a Jolly Good Fellow." It was one of the truly unforgettable moments in Wimbledon history.

"I always felt that I hadn't achieved what I wanted to achieve. I always felt I could get better."

—Virginia Wade

Evonne Goolagong

64

Evonne Goolagong

Maybe Goolagong's victory over the great Margaret Court in the 1971 Wimbledon ladies' singles final wasn't a complete surprise, given that Goolagong had just won her first Grand Slam singles title a month earlier in France, but the way in which she beat Court, dominating her 6–4, 6–1, was shocking. Goolagong, an athletic beauty of Australian aboriginal descent, lost to Billie Jean King in the finals the following year. Then, after marrying Roger Cawley in 1975, she came up short in two more finals, losing again to King in 1975 and Chris Evert in 1976, before winning her second Wimbledon singles title in 1980, defeating Evert-Lloyd (who had married John Lloyd), 6–1, 7–6. With this victory, she became the first mother to win at Wimbledon since Dorothea Lambert Chambers in 1914. Goolagong-Cawley also captured two ladies' doubles titles, in 1974 and 1977.

65

Strawberries and Cream

Apparently, the British are quite fond of strawberries. At least when it comes to Wimbledon they are. Every day, some 2,000 kilos of strawberries with 7,000 liters of cream are served at The Championships. The Grade 1 strawberries, grown in Kent, are picked the day before they are served and trucked directly to Wimbledon to guarantee freshness.

"To see her play was like watching a deer leaping across the veldt or a tiger pouncing on its prey."

—John Barrett on Evonne Goolagong, *Wimbledon: The Official History of the Championships*

66

Björn Borg

The "Ice Man" from Sweden was one of the great tennis players of all time. Sporting long, blond locks tamed by his signature Fila headband, and a scruffy beard, Borg dominated the grass courts at Wimbledon like no man since William Renshaw, winning five consecutive singles titles from 1976 through 1980—a record for the Open era that was recently tied by Roger Federer. The ultimate baseliner, with machine-like consistency and stamina, Borg dismantled Ilie Nastase in straight sets for his first title and followed that with two consecutive finals defeats of Jimmy Connors. In 1979, Roscoe Tanner stretched Borg to five sets and actually held a two-sets-to-one lead before falling victim to Borg's overall superiority. Then came one of the classic matches of all time: Borg's 1980 victory over John McEnroe, 1–6, 7–5, 6–3, 6–7, 8–6, featuring a 34-point fourth-set tie break won by McEnroe, 18–16. In 1981, Borg recovered from a two-set deficit to Jimmy Connors in the semifinals and had a chance at a sixth consecutive title, but McEnroe ended the streak with a 4–6, 7–6, 7–6, 6–4 win. Still, Borg retired with 11 Grand Slam singles titles—five at Wimbledon and six at the French Open—and a record 41-match winning streak at Wimbledon.

Bjorn Borg, 1978
Inset, Borg in 1979

The Tie Break

Björn Borg, vying for his fifth consecutive Wimbledon singles title, and first-time finalist John McEnroe put on a show for the ages in the 1980 men's final. The 21-year-old McEnroe easily won the first set 6–1, but Borg fought back and took a two-sets-to-one lead. In the fourth set, Borg broke McEnroe to lead 5–4 and served for the match. But McEnroe broke back; then both held serve to force a tie break at 6–6. Back and forth they went, with Borg serving for the match at 6–5 and 7–6. McEnroe refused to surrender and held two set points of his own. He also failed to convert, and it was Borg's turn again. But the Swede couldn't produce a winner on three straight chances, and McEnroe regained the momentum. Four more times McEnroe tried to finish off the set, but Borg held on. Finally, after 22 minutes and 34 points, McEnroe won the tie break, 18–16, to square the match. In the final set, Borg's steely nerves and superior stamina proved too much for McEnroe, and Borg claimed his fifth consecutive title.

John McEnroe, 1980

> *"This was violently exciting tennis.... The speed of the shots and reaction, racket-handling and timing were breathtaking."*
>
> — Rex Bellamy, *The Times*

68

John McEnroe

He could be an obnoxious brat, prone to temperamental outbursts on the court, but McEnroe was also a brilliant tennis player. When McEnroe was at his best, he was a shotmaking artist with a superb serve-and-volley game. For five years running, from 1980 through 1984, McEnroe made it to the men's singles final, winning three times. His first visit ended in a heartbreaking loss to Björn Borg in the famous "Tie Break" match of 1980. In 1981, McEnroe ended the Swede's five-year reign as Wimbledon champ with a four-set victory. Jimmy Connors outlasted McEnroe in five sets in 1982. Then McEnroe went on to win two consecutive titles in 1983 and 1984, demolishing both Chris Lewis and Connors in straight sets, never losing more than two games in any set. McEnroe also won five men's doubles titles—four with Peter Fleming between 1979 and 1984, and his fifth in 1992 with Michael Stich, in a memorable match with Jim Grabb and Richey Reneberg. McEnroe and Stich finally prevailed in the fifth set, 19–17.

"He is a young man who raised perfectly placed strokes to a high art form, only to resort to tantrums that smear his masterpieces like graffiti."

—Pete Axthelm, *Newsweek*

69

You Cannot Be Serious!

McEnroe is as well known for his ferocious outbursts on the court as he is for his championships. These outbursts were especially disturbing at Wimbledon, a place that prides itself on its traditions and decorum. McEnroe claimed the umpires were out to get him, but his temper tantrums rarely seemed to affect his play. In fact, George Plimpton once commented in an article for *Esquire* magazine that McEnroe was "the only player in the history of the game to go berserk and play better tennis." Perhaps his best-known outburst was in a first-round match against Tom Gullikson in 1981. Disputing the umpire's call, McEnroe went into a tirade, screaming "You can't be serious, man! You CANNOT be serious! That ball was on the line! Chalk flew up! It was clearly in! How can you possibly call that out? Now he's [Gullikson] walking over! Everyone knows it's in in the whole stadium, and you call it out? You guys are the absolute pits of the world, you know that?" In response to McEnroe's bitter harangue, umpire Edward James stoically penalized McEnroe a point. But McEnroe had the last laugh, winning the match and, later, the men's singles title.

70

The Umpires

More than 300 officials from around the world, but primarily from Britain, serve as umpires during The Championships. Each match has one chair umpire and two line teams that work in 75-minute shifts. It's not an easy job, to say the least, requiring absolute focus, sometimes at one's own peril. On occasion, the umpires are verbally abused by the players and can be subject to inadvertent physical injury from a speeding ball or lunging player. Still, they remain steadfast in their duties, a critical cog in a well-oiled machine.

71

Ball Boys and Girls

You see them scrambling after loose balls at the end of points or missed serves. Quick as rabbits darting across a meadow, they clear the court while attempting to be as unobtrusive as possible. These ball boys and girls serve an essential function at The Championships, keeping the matches running smoothly. It's a great honor for the lucky 200 or so who are selected from the local schools each year after a rather rigorous examination period. Originally only boys served this function. Girls joined the crew in 1977 but were not used on Centre Court until 1985.

"These ball boys are marvellous. You don't even notice them. There's a left-handed one over there. I noticed him earlier."

—Max Robertson, commentator

Martina Navratilova

Navratilova, arguably the best woman ever to play the game, was the queen of Wimbledon. She won a record nine—that's right, nine—ladies' singles titles, including an incredible six in a row from 1982 through 1987. After back-to-back losses to Steffi Graf in 1988 and 1989, Navratilova won her last Wimbledon singles title in 1990 at the age of 33, defeating Zina Garrison in straight sets. She then had a chance at a seemingly impossible 10th singles title in 1994, but lost to Conchita Martínez in straight sets. As she left Centre Court, following her record 12th singles final, Navratilova stooped to pluck a few blades of grass to keep as a memento of her time there.

And the titles didn't stop there. Navratilova won seven ladies' doubles championships—five with Pam Shriver, including four in a row from 1981 through 1984. And she also won four mixed doubles titles, spanning an 18-year period from 1985 to 2003. Her 2003 championship, with partner Leander Paes, made her the oldest winner of any Grand Slam title at the age of 46 years, 8 months. It also tied her with Billie Jean King for the most titles at Wimbledon, with 20. Navratilova's total of 58 Grand Slam titles overall is second only to Margaret Court in the history of the game.

Martina Navratilova collecting a few blades of grass as a souvenir from Centre Court following her finals match with Conchita Martinez, 1994

"There never will be another Chris and Martina show. There never was another like it and there never will be another."

—Martina Navratilova

73

Martina and Chrissy

It's a rivalry that knows no equal in tennis and is one of the greatest individual rivalries in the history of sport. For fifteen years, Martina Navratilova and Chris Evert, two of the best players in women's tennis history, battled each other, and nowhere was the battle more fierce than on the grass courts at Wimbledon. Evert might have owned the clay in Paris, but Martina built her legacy on grass. Five times they met in the ladies' singles final at Wimbledon, and each time when it was over, Navratilova clutched the champion's trophy.

Their first meeting, in 1978, is considered one of the great finals of all time. Evert took advantage of Navratilova's nerves and raced to a one-set advantage, winning the opener 6–2. But Navratilova used her superb serve-and-volley game to capture the next two sets, 6–4, 7–5, and her first singles title. Thus began a streak of unprecedented dominance by Navratilova at The Championships.

While there was no love lost when they were on opposite sides of the net, they had great respect for each other and over time became good friends. Early on, they even teamed up to win the women's doubles title at Wimbledon, knocking off Billie Jean King and Betty Stove in the finals in 1976.

74

A Colorful History

Dark green and purple are the official colors of Wimbledon — a unique and somewhat curious choice. It's also a bit peculiar that in a place so steeped in tradition, no one seems to know why this particular combination was chosen way back in 1909. Originally, the club sported a blue, yellow, red, and green combo, but it was deemed too similar to the Royal Marines and the decision was made to move to the current pairing, which can be found just about everywhere at the All England Club, from the logo adorning the official merchandise to the umpire's neckties.

Boris Becker

The Flying Deutscheman

Boris Becker fearlessly flung himself around the court without any apparent concern for the consequences. This untamed aggressiveness made the young German a fan favorite and one of the best ever to grace the lawns of Wimbledon. In 1985, unseeded and only 17 years old, Becker won the 99th men's singles championship over Kevin Curren in four sets, making Becker the youngest male and first unseeded winner of Wimbledon. He won again in 1986, with a straight-set victory over top seed Ivan Lendl.

For three consecutive years, from 1988 through 1990, Becker and Stefan Edberg met in the men's singles final. It marked the first time since the days of the Challenge Round that the same two men played each other in three straight finals. Edberg got the better of Becker in two of the three matches, winning in four sets in 1988 and five in 1990. Becker took the 1989 final in straight sets for his third title. The flying Deutscheman, who often prowled the courts with knees bloodied from his efforts, made the finals again in 1991 and 1995, but he failed to win a fourth title.

"I go to London, my favourite city in the world, and I feel at home."

—Boris Becker on Wimbledon

Steffi Graf

Steffi Graf

Graf showed great promise at her first Wimbledon, in 1984, at the tender age of 15. She motored through her first three matches and went down swinging in the fourth round to 10th-seeded Jo Durie, losing 9–7 in the third set. Three years later, Graf made her first final, losing to Martina Navratilova—Navratilova's sixth straight title. But that was when the tide turned. In 1988, Graf ended Navratilova's reign with an emphatic 5–7, 6–2, 6–1 victory in the championship match. Graf went on to win the Grand Slam that year and the Olympic gold medal, making her the only player ever to win the "Golden Slam."

Graf had one of the best forehands the game has ever seen, and her excellent court coverage made her that much tougher. She repeated her win over Navratilova in 1989 and went on to capture seven Wimbledon singles titles in nine years. Graf won 22 Grand Slam singles titles overall, and is the only player in history, male or female, to win each of the four Slams four times or more, making a strong case that she was the best ever.

77

Cashing In

When 11th-seeded Pat Cash upset number two seed Ivan Lendl in straight sets in the 1987 men's final, it marked the first time since John Newcombe's win in 1971 that an Australian man had won at Wimbledon. What made it more memorable was Cash's spirited climb to his family's box in the Centre Court stands. Cash's spontaneous celebration with his family and coach, Ian Barclay, has now become something of a tradition at Wimbledon as other champions have followed suit.

78

The Frosted Flake

Andre Agassi, who called himself "the Frosted Flake," admitted he wasn't comfortable with everything that is Wimbledon. In fact, the grass, among other things, gave him fits. But in 1992, on his third trip to The Championships, "the Las Vegas Lollipop," who was better known for his wild blond hair and colorful tennis garb, used his lethal passing shots to overcome his self-doubt—and 39 aces by Goran Ivanisevic—to win his only Wimbledon title, 6–7, 6–4, 6–4, 1–6, 6–4. For Agassi, it was a breakthrough win. Though he never won another Wimbledon title, he went on to capture eight Grand Slam titles overall. He married tennis legend Steffi Graf in 2001.

"If Agassi ever wins Wimbledon, I'll eat my T-shirt. Not only has he no chance to win, but if he doesn't pull himself together soon, he could be out of tennis in two or three years."

—Edwin Pope, *Miami Herald* sports editor, 1992

Andre Agassi

79

People's Sunday

Normally, no matches are played on the middle Sunday of The Championships, but occasionally weather delays force officials to schedule matches on this traditional day of rest. It's happened only three times in history, in 1991, 1997, and 2004. When this occurs, tickets are made available to the general public at reduced pricing and seating is unreserved, as is the crowd at times. "People's Sunday" gives many who would not otherwise have the opportunity a chance to attend. If the conclusion of the tournament has to be extended beyond the traditional completion on the second Sunday, then the same standards apply on "People's Monday."

80

The Youth Movement

Jennifer Capriati was an amazing talent at an incredibly young age. After reaching the semifinals at the French Open in 1990 at the age of 14, Capriati was seeded 12th at Wimbledon—the youngest seeded player ever. She made it to the fourth round before falling to Steffi Graf. A year later, Capriati stunned defending champion Martina Navratilova in the quarterfinals—Navratilova hadn't lost that early at Wimbledon in 14 years. Capriati's win made her the youngest player ever to reach the semifinals at Wimbledon.

When Martina Hingis won the women's doubles title at Wimbledon with partner Helena Suková in 1996, she became the youngest player ever to win a Grand Slam title. At 15 years, 282 days, she was just three days younger than Lottie Dod, the previous record holder, who won her first ladies' singles title at Wimbledon in 1887. Hingis won the women's singles title in 1997 at the age of 16. She was also the victim of possibly the greatest upset in Wimbledon history when, as the number one seed, she lost to unseeded Jelena Dokic, 6–2, 6–0, in the opening round in 1999.

Fans show their support for Britain's Tim Henman, People's Sunday, 2004.

No. 1 Court

It's an honor and a privilege to play on any of Wimbledon's courts, but the prestige of playing on No. 1 Court is second only to a Centre Court match. In 1997, the All England Club opened the new No. 1 Court complex, replacing the old No. 1 Court, which had stood next to Centre Court since 1928. The new stadium seats 11,429 fans—an increase of more than 4,000—and includes restaurants, shops, and hospitality suites. The bowl-shaped venue, built into the hillside north of Centre Court, offers fans unobstructed views of the action. It's a wonderful place to enjoy a bowl of strawberries and cream while watching some spectacular tennis.

Nikolay Davydenko, right, and
Kevin Anderson on No. 1 Court, 2010

Tickets

Tickets to Wimbledon, especially those for Centre Court, are among the most coveted in all of sports. Debenture holders are given one ticket for every day of the championships. Tickets are also available to the public through a lottery system. The club reserves approximately 500 tickets per day for Centre Court (except for the last four days), No. 1 Court, and No. 2 Court, which are available on a first-come, first-served basis. These are very popular and induce long, overnight queues of devoted fans. Some 6,000 ground admission tickets are also made available each day, offering access to the secondary courts.

83

Aorangi Park

On a grassy hillside north of Centre Court is the popular spot known as Aorangi Park. Here, fans without tickets can watch live action on a large-screen TV while basking in the warm summer sun—when it chooses to make an appearance. Over the years, the press has given the park other nicknames, such as "Henman Hill" and "Murray Field," in reference to notable British players.

84

Tea Time

There's no shortage of beverage choices at Wimbledon. One of the most popular is a Pimms No. 1 Cup, a warm-weather favorite in Britain. Pimm's, a gin-based beverage with subtle flavors of citrus and spice, is topped with, for example, club soda, and served over ice with a cucumber slice and lemon wedge as garnish. Champagne is also quite popular. About 20,000 bottles are served each fortnight. That's a lot of bubbly!

Robinsons Lemon Barley Water is a popular soft drink choice. A mixture of water, fresh lemon juice, sugar, and Robinson's barley flour, it made its first appearance in 1935, when medical representative Eric Smedley Hodgson mixed the concoction and served it to competitors in the men's changing room. And, of course, if none of these strikes your fancy, there's always tea.

Pete Sampras

If Martina Navratilova is the queen of Wimbledon, then Sampras might just be the king. Pistol Pete won seven men's singles titles in eight years, between 1993 and 2000, tying William Renshaw's record for most ever. Only once in those seven finals was Sampras stretched to five sets, versus Goran Ivanisevic in 1998.

A great all-court player with a powerful serve and crushing, running forehand, Sampras was at his best on grass. His loss to eventual champion Richard Kracijek in the 1996 quarterfinals was Sampras' only defeat on the surface in 54 matches during his championship run. When he defeated Patrick Rafter for his seventh Wimbledon title in 2000, Sampras broke Roy Emerson's record for career Grand Slam singles titles by a man with his 13th. Sampras went on to extend his record to 14 when he won the 2002 U.S. Open. He is considered to be one of the greatest players of all time and possibly the best male ever on grass.

"This used to be my backyard. Now it belongs to Pete."

—Boris Becker

Pete Sampras

86
Lucky Number 13

When Pete Sampras came to Wimbledon in 2000, in search of his seventh men's singles title and record-breaking 13th Grand Slam singles championship, he was nursing a bad back. Things got significantly worse in the second round when tendinitis in his shin flared up, making every point an excruciating experience. Somehow, Sampras gutted out a four-set win over Karol Kucera, then willed himself to the final, losing only two more sets in the next four matches. On a dreary Sunday afternoon, battling 12th-seed Patrick Rafter, Sampras lost the first set in a tiebreaker and faced a 1–4 deficit in the second. That's when Sampras dug a little deeper, calling on all his experience from past finals, and stole the second set in a tiebreaker, then swept through the next two sets to win his record-breaking 13th Grand Slam singles title. As darkness began to fall over Centre Court, a teary-eyed Sampras climbed into the stands and hugged his parents while the packed house stood applauding his accomplishment.

"I love Wimbledon. This is the best court in the world. It's my home away from home."

—Pete Sampras

Pete Sampras hugs his father after his record-breaking win, 2000

Sander Lantinga showing off his footwear, among other things, on Centre Court, 2006

87
Streakers

It's not a completely uncommon occurrence for a fan to streak across Centre Court. Melissa Johnson showed her unabashed love of tennis by baring her chest and bottom to amused finalists Richard Kracijek and MaliVai Washington prior to the start of the 1996 men's final.

During the men's singles final in 2002 between Lleyton Hewitt and David Nalbandian, a male streaker put on quite a show. After theatrically tossing his shoes, he tumbled over the net and pranced around Centre Court for quite some time before being caught by security and escorted away in a bright red cloak.

In 2006, Dutch radio DJ Sander Lantinga elected to bare his soul, among other things, to Maria Sharapova and Elena Dementieva during a quarterfinal match. Sharapova turned her back as the young man boldly turned a cartwheel. Wonder if the exposure boosted his ratings?

88
The Wild Card

At the discretion of the competition committee, players who have not otherwise qualified for The Championships can be granted a wild card entry into the tournament. Since the practice was initiated in 1977, only one wild card has won a singles title: Goran Ivanisevic in 2001. And the finals match, played on People's Monday before a raucous crowd, was one of the unforgettable moments in Wimbledon history.

Three-time finals loser Ivanisevic faced equally popular Patrick Rafter, runner-up the previous year. The match was one for the ages, with the two gladiators trading blows and sets for three hours, until the unseeded Ivanisevic won the deciding set 9–7. The crowd was delirious with joy. At last the holder of the Grand Slam trophy he so deserved, Ivanisevic climbed atop the TV commentators' box to salute his fans.

89
At the Movies

A few years back, a local multiscreen movie complex in Wimbledon came up with its own method for rating films. Instead of the usual age-based ratings used in England, tennis personalities were substituted. English favorite Tim Henman was chosen to represent unrestricted (family-friendly) films. The Williams sisters, Venus and Serena, were chosen for the PG rating since their father is seemingly always with them. Anna Kournikova, the pretty girl clad in skimpy outfits, garnered the 15+ rating, while infamous bad boy John McEnroe got the 18+ rating for his excessive use of foul language and violent outbursts.

90
Hawk Eyes

In 2000, after seeing his exploits on television, Wimbledon officials brought in Hamish, a live hawk owned by Avian Control Systems, to help persuade trespassing pigeons to find feeding grounds and accommodations away from the famed grass courts. Fearing the predator, the pigeons fled to safer surroundings. In return for their services, Hamish and, more recently, Rufus received official tournament passes bearing their photograph.

Rufus

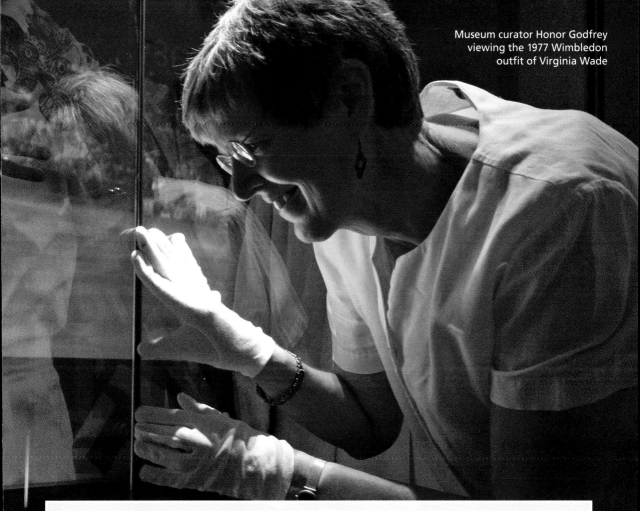

91

The Lawn Tennis Museum

In 2006, the Wimbledon Lawn Tennis Museum opened to the public. Inside are exhibits that chronicle the history of tennis, an amazing collection of memorabilia, and a 200-degree cinema where visitors can watch a film on the science of tennis. They also can view the Championship Trophies, visit a library specifically dedicated to lawn tennis, shop, and grab a bite in the café. It's open year-round, but only ticket holders can visit during The Championships.

The Williams Sisters

Venus and Serena, the Williams sisters, are incredible, physically gifted athletes who have changed women's tennis, bringing a combination of power and finesse to the court that previously did not exist. Since Venus' first ladies' singles title in 2000, the two sisters have dominated Centre Court, combining to win nine of eleven championships, through 2010. Venus' win in 2000 was also the first time an African American woman had won at Wimbledon since Althea Gibson in 1958.

Venus has won five titles, in 2000, 2001, 2005, 2007, and 2008, making her the most accomplished woman on grass since Steffi Graf. Her 4–6, 7–6, 9–7 victory over Lindsay Davenport in the 2005 final is the longest women's finals match in Wimbledon history, at 2 hours 45 minutes, and is regarded as one of the greatest matches ever. Serena has won four titles, in 2002, 2003, 2009, and 2010. The first three came against her sister. Venus has beaten Serena just once in a Wimbledon final, in 2008. The sisters have also won four ladies' doubles titles at Wimbledon, in 2000, 2002, 2008, and 2009. They have not lost a set in those four finals.

"Family's first, and that's what matters most. We realize that our love goes deeper than the tennis game."

—Serena Williams

Venus Williams serving to Serena Williams, 2009

Roger Federer

Roger Federer

It is quite likely that when his career finally comes to an end, Federer will go down as the best tennis player ever. No one achieves a record like his without a complete all-court game, but it's Federer's forehand that has elevated him to greatness. That and his uncanny ability to consistently win the key points in the biggest matches.

From 2003 to 2009, Federer won six Wimbledon men's singles titles in seven years, his only loss coming in the 2008 final to Rafael Nadal, in one of the classic matches in tennis history. The five in a row he won from 2003 to 2007 match Björn Borg's modern-day record. Federer also holds the men's record for most Grand Slam singles titles, with 16 through 2010, and made the semifinals or better in 23 consecutive Grand Slam events from 2004 to 2010. Between 2005 and 2007, Federer made the finals in 10 consecutive Slam events, another record. Three times, in 2004, 2006, and 2007, he won three of the four Grand Slam singles titles in the same year. It's hard to argue that any other man was better.

"In an era of specialists, you're either a clay court specialist, a grass court specialist, or a hard court specialist...or you're Roger Federer."

—Jimmy Connors

"*Federer's sublime technique was matched by Nadal's blistering strength as the sun went down over Centre Court....On this occasion, beauty lost out to the beast.*"

—Gerard Meagher, morethanthegames.co.uk

Rafael Nadal celebrating his
win over Roger Federer, 2008

The Greatest Match Ever

Roger Federer was already the three-time defending champion when he first met Rafael Nadal in the 2006 men's final at Wimbledon. Federer won that one fairly easily, in four sets. But in 2007, Nadal stretched Federer to the limit, with the Swiss champ outlasting the young Spaniard in the fifth set, 6–2, in a match that was memorable in its own right. However, that was just a prelude to what is widely considered the greatest match of all time — the 2008 men's singles final.

The two combatants pounded each other for nearly five hours, with rain delays extending the total match time to more than seven hours. Nadal looked likely to unseat the five-time champ early on, winning the first two sets, 6–4, 6–4, and going up a break in the third. But Federer dug deep, broke back, and then stole the third set in a tiebreaker. When Federer won the fourth set in another tiebreaker, 7–6 (10–8), it looked like the championship was slipping from Nadal's grasp. Still full of fight, however, Nadal traded game after game with his rival and finally broke Federer in the rapidly fading light, capturing the fifth set, 9–7, to win his first Wimbledon title and end Federer's record-tying streak at five.

Roger Federer serving
to Andy Roddick, 2009

95

Federer Versus Roddick

One year removed from Rafael Nadal's epic, five-set win over Roger Federer, American Andy Roddick strolled onto Centre Court hoping to duplicate Nadal's feat. Roddick, who had previously lost to Federer in the 2004 and 2005 finals, won the first set, 7–5, and held four set points in the second-set tiebreaker. But he failed to convert any, and Federer won six straight points to take the tiebreaker and even the match. A Federer ace, one of 50 in the match, closed out the third set in another tiebreaker, but Roddick fought back to even the match at two sets apiece with a 6–3 victory in the fourth. The fifth set was remarkable. Federer and Roddick pounded serve after serve, ace after ace, with neither giving an inch. Into the 30th game of the set—yes, the set—they went without a service break. With Roddick serving for the 39th time in the match, Federer finally broke the unrelenting American and won his 15th Grand Slam singles title, breaking Pete Sampras' record. It was the only service Roddick lost all day.

96

Centre Court

It is the quintessential venue in tennis—the one place every player dreams of playing. This ivy-clad structure, so steeped in history and tradition, now sports a more modern feel. Centre Court opened in 1922, when the club moved to its present location on Church Road. A recent renovation expanded the number of seats to 15,000, and a new roof was put in place. The larger opening allows more sunlight to reach the famed court, while the state-of-the-art retractable roof protects the court, players, officials, and fans from the rain. Centre Court is reserved for matches featuring the best and most popular players in the earlier rounds, as well as the semifinals, finals, and, of course, the trophy presentations to the champions.

97

Triumph and Disaster

A quote from Kipling's poem "If—" hangs above the players' entrance to Centre Court. It reads, "If you can meet with Triumph and Disaster and treat those two imposters just the same."

Jeremy Chardy, left, and Andy Roddick doing battle on Centre Court, 2009

Marathon Men

There has never been anything like it in the history of tennis, and likely never will be again. On Tuesday, June 22, 2010, John Isner and Nicolas Mahut seemed to be playing another hard-fought yet somewhat innocuous first-round match on Court 18. Tied at two sets apiece, the match was suspended due to darkness, and they resumed play on Wednesday. When Mahut held serve to tie the fifth set at 6–6, little did anyone know what was to follow. Seven hours passed, with each man holding serve, until the match was again suspended because of darkness, with the score tied at 59. The two warriors resumed the battle on Thursday and played another hour before Isner finally broke Mahut to win the set, 70–68. That's right, 70–68! In total, the match lasted 11 hours 5 minutes. The fifth set alone lasted 8 hours 11 minutes, more than two hours longer than the longest match ever. Isner and Mahut combined to serve 215 aces and held serve for 168 straight games.

> "We played the greatest match ever in the greatest place to play tennis."
>
> —Nicolas Mahut

John Isner, left, Nicolas Mahut, center, and Chair Umpire Mohamed Lahyani

99

The Venus Rosewater Dish

Since 1886, this trophy has been presented to the ladies' singles champion. The sterling silver dish, trimmed in gold, features a mythology-based design copied from a pewter dish dating to the 1500s that now resides in the Louvre. Presented by the Duchess of Kent, the original trophy remains in the possession of the All England Club, housed in the Wimbledon Lawn Tennis Museum. The winner receives an eight-inch replica for her trophy case, a generous check, and a lifetime membership in the club.

100

The Single-Handed Champion of the World

The men's singles champion is awarded the Gentlemen's Singles Trophy, inscribed with "The All England Lawn Tennis Club Single-Handed Championship of the World." A pineapple sits atop the cover of the double-handled silver gilt cup, and heads sporting winged helmets support the handles at their base. It's a classic trophy design, beautiful and elegant, worthy of the traditional kiss from the champion. Like the women's trophy, after the presentation, the original is returned to the museum and the winner receives a miniature replica — plus a rather hefty sum of money and a lifetime membership in the club.

Rafael Nadal, 2010

Victory

Wimbledon. It's the ultimate championship in tennis—on par with the Super Bowl, the World Cup, and Olympic gold. It's played on the most hallowed grounds in the sport, and victory here defines a player's place in history and reminds us all, each year, of the importance of strength, perseverance, sportsmanship, and achievement. And nowhere does it mean more than on Centre Court at the All England Club.

Serena Williams, 2009

John Isner and Nicolas Mahut, 2010